DO THE WORK OF AN EVANGELIST
A MANUAL FOR BOLD WITNESS

ABRAHAM JT HARRIS

Copyright © 2025 by Abraham JT Harris

All rights reserved.

No portion of this book may be reproduced in any form without written permission from the publisher or author, except as permitted by U.S. copyright law.

Scripture quotations identified from the Holy Bible, New International Version. NIV. Copyright @ 2012 by YouVersionBibleApp. YouVersion.com

Scripture quotations identified from the Holy Bible, New Living Translation. NLT. Copyright @ 2012 by YouVersionBibleApp. YouVersion.com

Scripture quotations identified from the Holy Bible, New King James. NKJV. Copyright @ 2012 by YouVersionBibleApp. YouVersion.com

Scripture quotations identified from the Holy Bible, King James Version. KJV. Copyright @ 2012 by YouVersionBibleApp. YouVersion.com

Scripture quotations identified from the Holy Bible, English Standard Version. ESV. Copyright @ 2012 by YouVersionBibleApp. YouVersion.com

Contents

Introduction: Evangelist: A Manual for Bold Witness — 1

1. The Call to Evangelize — 3
2. What Is an Evangelist? — 6
3. The Heart of the Evangelist — 10
4. The Gospel Message — 15
5. Preparation for Evangelism — 20
6. Power Evangelism — 25
7. One-on-One Soul-Winning — 31
8. Street and Public Evangelism — 37
9. Evangelism in the Local Church — 44
10. Digital Evangelism — 51
11. Follow-Up and Discipleship — 57
12. The Rewards and the Cost — 64
13. Evangelism and Revival — 70
14. Raising Up Evangelists — 76
15. The Urgency of the Hour — 82

30 Powerful Principles for Evangelists Traveling to Preach — 87

| 31-Day Evangelist's Reading Plan: "Burning for the Lost" | 92 |
| Author's Page | 98 |

Introduction: Evangelist: A Manual for Bold Witness

We are not living in ordinary times. The urgency of the hour is clear—darkness is increasing, deception is spreading, and people everywhere are searching for truth, hope, and salvation. But God has always had a response to darkness: a messenger. From Noah to Paul, from Peter in Jerusalem to evangelists in every generation, God raises up men and women who are willing to speak boldly, live righteously, and proclaim Jesus without shame.

This manual is for those who feel the tug of heaven on their heart. It's for the street preacher, the missionary, the church planter, the revivalist, the one-on-one soul winner, and the person burning with a desire to see the lost come home. Whether you're new to evangelism or a seasoned laborer, Evangelist: A Manual for Bold Witness will equip you with biblical wisdom, practical tools, and prophetic fire to fulfill your calling.

In these pages, you'll discover:

- What it truly means to be an evangelist—not just a preacher of sermons, but a carrier of the burden of souls.

- How to preach with power, not performance.

- How to navigate spiritual warfare, rejection, and persecution with grace and authority.

- The role of prayer, purity, and the power of the Holy Spirit in evangelistic ministry.

- Strategies for personal soul-winning, crusades, team evangelism, digital outreach, and follow-up.

- How to build lasting fruit, not just emotional moments.

Evangelism is not a side ministry of the church—it is the front line. The gospel is still the power of God unto salvation, and there is no backup plan. We don't need better entertainment. We need better evangelists—those who walk in the fear of God, carry the compassion of Christ, and speak with the authority of the Holy Spirit.

This is a call back to the raw, real, and Spirit-led ministry of Jesus. The ministry that sat with sinners, challenged religious systems, cast out demons, healed the broken, and preached the kingdom with power. The ministry that goes to the highways and byways, not just to the platforms and pulpits.

Let this book be your training ground, your companion, and your fire-starter. Read it with an open Bible and an open heart. Take notes, pray over the pages, let it ignite your passion again—or for the first time.

The fields are white for harvest. The Holy Spirit is still sending. The gospel is still enough.

You were born for this.

Now go—preach, reach, and reap.

Chapter 1
The Call to Evangelize

The command to preach the Gospel did not originate from man—it came from the risen Christ Himself. Before Jesus ascended to the right hand of the Father, He gave His followers a divine charge that echoes through generations. He did not suggest, recommend, or propose—He commissioned. Evangelism is not an optional activity reserved for the passionate few; it is the marching order of the entire Church.

The Final Words of Jesus Still Stand

In Matthew 28, Jesus spoke with heavenly authority:

"I have been given all authority in heaven and on earth. Therefore, go and make disciples of all the nations..."

(Matthew 28:18–19 NLT)

This was no casual comment whispered to a few. It was a heavenly declaration. Jesus, now reigning over all, was saying in effect, "Because I rule over everything, you now move forward under My authority." The command to go was not attached to convenience, personality, or gifting—it was rooted in obedience.

In Mark 16, the command carries power and urgency:

"Go into all the world and preach the Good News to everyone. Anyone who believes and is baptized will be saved..."

(Mark 16:15–16 NLT)

These were the parting words of the One who had conquered sin, death, and hell. They are not suggestions to consider—they are our mission. And that mission still stands today.

Jesus didn't say, "Wait until you feel ready." He said, "Go." He didn't say, "Only go if you're a preacher." He said, "Go into all the world." That includes classrooms, workplaces, neighborhoods, and nations. The Gospel was never meant to stay confined within church walls. It was born to move through people.

Paul's Charge to Timothy: Do the Work

Years after the ascension, the apostle Paul—aware that his time was short—wrote a final charge to his spiritual son, Timothy. These words ring with urgency and clarity:

"But you, keep a clear mind in every situation. Don't be afraid of suffering for the Lord. Work at telling others the Good News, and fully carry out the ministry God has given you."
(2 Timothy 4:5 NLT)

This wasn't written to a traveling evangelist. It was addressed to a pastor—but more than that, to a disciple. Paul wasn't calling Timothy to a platform, but to faithfulness. He told him to work at evangelism—to labor in it, prioritize it, and give it his all. Evangelism takes intentionality, endurance, and grit. It's not always convenient or glamorous. It's spiritual warfare, and it demands spiritual stamina.

Notice Paul's phrasing: "Work at telling others the Good News." That reminds us: evangelism doesn't happen by accident. It requires effort, focus, and fire.

Every Believer Is a Messenger

One of the greatest lies that's crippled the Church is that evangelism is for "ministers." But Scripture is clear: every follower of Jesus is a representative of the Gospel. You may never hold a microphone, but you carry a message. You may never stand on a stage, but you walk through fields of souls every day.

Jesus didn't save us just to sit—He saved us to send.

The early Church didn't explode because of one apostle. It grew because ordinary believers were filled with the Spirit and opened their mouths. When persecution scattered them, they didn't hide—they preached. And the Gospel spread like wildfire because they saw themselves as witnesses, not spectators.

You're not waiting for a green light—you've already been sent. Your life isn't on pause while others do the work. Your life is the work. You are the light of the world. You are salt in a decaying culture. You carry the answer, and His name is Jesus.

No More Excuses

This is the hour to lay down excuses. Whether you're an introvert or extrovert, seasoned or new, young or old—if you have the Holy Spirit, you have all you need to obey the call. The harvest is not lacking souls—it's lacking laborers.

Jesus is not looking for the most eloquent, but the most available.

This chapter is your summons—not from a man, but from God. You are called to evangelize. Not later—now. Not once you feel perfect—but because the need is urgent. You have something the world desperately needs. And God wants to use your voice, your story, and your obedience to bring souls into His Kingdom.

Chapter 2
What Is an Evangelist?

Understanding the Gift, the Call, and the Office

The Church today doesn't just need more noise—it needs clarity. While many are stirred to share their faith, there's often confusion about what it actually means to be an evangelist. Is it a title? A spiritual gift? A lifestyle? A ministry office? Scripture doesn't leave us in the dark. It gives us real people, real assignments, and real authority placed on those who carry the message of Christ with fire, focus, and fruit.

Evangelists in Scripture: Ordinary People, Eternal Impact

One of the clearest examples of an evangelist in the New Testament is Philip. He wasn't one of the original Twelve Apostles. Yet Acts 8 tells us that when he entered Samaria, the city was shaken. He proclaimed Christ boldly. Demons were cast out. The paralyzed were healed. And joy flooded the region—not because of smoke machines or stage shows, but because one man brought the undiluted Gospel with power.

But Philip wasn't just used in the crowds. He was also led by the Spirit to a quiet desert road, where he encountered a single Ethiopian official. There were no microphones, no audience—just one man hungry for truth. Philip opened the Scriptures, preached Jesus, and baptized him. That moment in the desert had just as much weight in heaven as the public miracles. Why? Because a true evangelist obeys God in both the public and the private. It's not about numbers—it's about souls.

Jesus is the model Evangelist. He went from city to city, from house to house, preaching the kingdom, healing the sick, confronting darkness, and loving the unlovable. He didn't only minister to the masses—He took time for Nicodemus, the woman at the well, and Zacchaeus in a tree. His Gospel was clear: "Repent, for the Kingdom of God is at hand." It was not watered down, nor was it restrained. Jesus embodied the message and the mission.

And then there's Paul. Though primarily known as an apostle, Paul's evangelistic passion burned deep. He crossed borders, endured beatings, reasoned in synagogues, preached in marketplaces, and wept over souls. Paul didn't merely plant churches—he pursued lost people. He preached Christ in season and out of season, and never lost the fire of soul-winning. He showed us that evangelism isn't a season—it's a calling.

Gift. Office. Call.

In modern language, these terms often get blurred. But biblically, they each carry distinct meaning.

- The Call to Evangelize is for everyone. Every follower of Jesus is called to share the Gospel. Whether it's across a pulpit or across a lunch table, this is the basic call of every believer—to make Jesus known.

- The Gift of Evangelism is given by the Holy Spirit to certain individuals. These believers may not be in full-time ministry, but there's a supernatural effectiveness and boldness that follows their witness. They're soul-sensitive. They carry a burden for the lost and often lead many to Christ.

- The Office of the Evangelist is a leadership role established by Christ. Ephesians 4:11 lists evangelists among the five-fold ministry gifts—apostles, prophets, evangelists, pastors, and teachers. This office is not based on human appointment or personal ambition—it is a divine placement. Evangelists in this office do more than win souls; they equip the Church to win souls. They stir revival, break spiritual apathy, and partner with the other ministry gifts to advance the Kingdom.

When someone stands in the office of the evangelist, their entire life is shaped by that mission. They live to proclaim the cross. They labor to see conversions. They carry a message that both wounds and heals—confronting sin, calling to repentance, and proclaiming the mercy of God. And their fruit is unmistakable.

The Evangelist in the Five-Fold Ministry
Paul writes in **Ephesians 4:11–12:**
"Now these are the gifts Christ gave to the church: the apostles, the prophets, the evangelists, and the pastors and teachers.
Their responsibility is to equip God's people to do His work and build up the church..." (NLT)

The evangelist is not a spiritual freelancer or a platform personality. They are part of the leadership structure Jesus Himself established. The apostle builds. The prophet reveals. The pastor shepherds. The teacher grounds. The evangelist gathers. They are uniquely graced to call for a response—to rally the lost, ignite the lukewarm, and mobilize the Church to go.

But they don't stop at altar calls. True evangelists equip. They train others to overcome fear, share boldly, and step out in faith. They mentor. They multiply. They break chains of complacency in the Church and impart the urgency of eternity.

When the evangelist is missing or misunderstood, churches become passive and introverted. But when the evangelist is recognized and released, the Church comes alive with mission and movement. We stop keeping the light under a bowl—and we let it shine.

Called or Commissioned—You're Not Left Out

Whether or not you carry the office, you still carry the call. You may never hold a microphone, but your mouth still matters. Evangelists aren't just seen in revival tents—they're found in break rooms, bus stops, board meetings, and city streets. Some will preach to thousands. Others will reach the one. But the value of a soul never changes.

You don't need a title to obey Jesus. You just need a heart that burns.

So let this chapter settle something in your spirit: You are not disqualified. You are not disqualified by your past, your personality, or your present stage of life. You have been called. You have been commissioned. And if you're willing to open your mouth, the Holy Spirit will fill it.

Let's reach the one. Let's reach the many. Let's take the Gospel out of the building and into the world.

Chapter 3
The Heart of the Evangelist

The Fire, the Burden, and the Compassion of Christ

You can be trained, gifted, eloquent, and even anointed—but if you don't carry the heart of God, your words will echo like noise without power. Evangelism is not a performance—it's a burden. It's not a career—it's a commission. And it doesn't begin on a platform—it begins in the secret place, where God places His heart within yours.

Love for Souls

Evangelists don't just carry a message—they carry a heartbeat. And the heartbeat of true evangelism is not strategy or charisma—it's love. Not a generic love. Not a theoretical love. But a deep, Spirit-born compassion that drives a person to action.

Jesus modeled this perfectly. Before He ever preached the Sermon on the Mount or raised the dead, Scripture says He was **"moved with compassion." (Matthew 9:36).** His compassion moved Him toward people others avoided. He touched the leper. He embraced the broken. He defended the woman caught in adultery. He saw beyond their sin—He saw their soul.

True evangelists weep before they speak. They intercede before they invite. They feel the weight of eternity behind every conversation, every outreach, every opportunity. You cannot effectively evangelize until you first ask God to break your heart for what breaks His.

You must see people the way He sees them. Not as obstacles. Not as statistics. But as eternal souls desperately in need of rescue. When the addict walks by, the evangelist doesn't look away—they look with love. When the atheist speaks with bitterness, the evangelist doesn't argue—they listen with mercy. When the backslider hides in shame, the evangelist doesn't condemn—they call them home.

This is the foundation: a heart full of the love of Christ.

Compassion Over Condemnation

You'll never win someone you've already written off.

Evangelists are not culture critics or angry moralists. They are messengers of hope. They do not shout at darkness from a distance—they step into it carrying the light. Their words may pierce, but not to destroy—to heal. Their message may convict, but it always carries the invitation of redemption.

The posture of the evangelist must mirror the posture of Christ: **"For God did not send His Son into the world to condemn the world, but to save the world through Him." (John 3:17 NLT)**

Yes, evangelists must speak truth. But truth without love becomes noise. It becomes a weapon instead of a lifeline. You may be doctrinally right, but if your tone is wrong, your message will fall flat. We're not called to preach against people—we're called to preach Christ to people.

Some people think that preaching hard means yelling louder. But real boldness isn't volume—it's clarity with compassion. It's confronting sin because you love. It's calling for repentance not to expose, but to restore. If the goal is just to be right, you've missed the heart of the Gospel. But if the goal is redemption—you're walking in the steps of Jesus.

Let this be your daily prayer:

"Lord, give me tears again. Let me feel the burden. Let me see what You see. Let me never become numb to the lost, indifferent to the broken, or judgmental toward the very people You died for."

Praying for the Burden of the Lord

True evangelism isn't birthed in classrooms or conferences—it's birthed in prayer. The burden of the Lord cannot be taught. It must be caught. You can't fabricate it. You can't fake it. You can only receive it from the presence of God.

This burden is holy. It is weighty. It's the ache that wakes you in the night. The tears that come without warning. The longing that rises in you when you see a crowd and wonder how many know Jesus. It's the fire that won't let you quit, even when you feel weary and unseen.

Jeremiah captured it best:

"His word burns in my heart like a fire, a fire shut up in my bones. I am worn out trying to hold it in! I can't do it!"
(Jeremiah 20:9 NLT)

That is the cry of the evangelist. Not "I have to preach," but "I can't stay silent." This burden consumes you. It ruins you for ordinary living. It changes how you pray, how you plan, how you spend, how you dream. You stop asking, "What do I want to do?" and start asking, "What does Heaven need from me?"

This is what separates event-based evangelism from eternal evangelism. One can be done out of routine. The other is done out of fire. One fades. The other costs you everything. But it also fills you with purpose, passion, and power.

When you carry God's burden, He will entrust you with His anointing.

The Heart of Jesus in the Evangelist
The heart of the evangelist must be the heart of Jesus:
- It leaves the 99 for the one.
- It looks for the prodigal on the road.
- It sees Zacchaeus in the tree.
- It hears the cry of Bartimaeus on the roadside.
- It tells the woman at the well, "I am the Messiah."
- It says to the thief on the cross, "Today, you'll be with Me in Paradise."

This is not poetic—it's prophetic. It is the actual posture of Christ. And it must be the posture of every person who dares to carry His Gospel. If you preach without His heart, you may draw a crowd but you'll miss the Kingdom.

Don't Just Preach—Burn
The world has heard enough empty preaching. It has seen enough shallow presentations. What it needs are flames. Men and women whose hearts are on fire. Not just with doctrine, but with love. Not just with theology, but with tears.

Don't just preach—burn. Don't just announce—intercede. Don't just speak truth—weep for souls. Because the fire in your bones will do more than your rehearsed sermon ever could.

You don't need to be polished—you need to be pierced. You don't need to be perfect—you need to be present with the burden of the Lord.

Evangelism doesn't begin with a microphone. It begins with a burdened heart—broken for the lost, burning with love, and bound by the call of God

Chapter 4
The Gospel Message

The Power, Clarity, and Call of the Cross

There is no evangelism without the Gospel. And there is no salvation without the message of the cross. We are not ambassadors of opinions, culture, or self-help. We are heralds of the Good News. And "good news" is exactly what the Gospel means—news that breaks chains, awakens hearts, cleanses consciences, and announces that hope has a name: Jesus.

But this message is not vague. It is not open to reinvention. It cannot be repackaged to suit trends or diluted to please crowds. The Gospel is the bold, confrontational, liberating truth of Jesus Christ—crucified for our sins, buried in a borrowed tomb, risen with power, ascended in glory, and soon to return.

This is not an idea. It is not a movement. It is not a suggestion. It is the power of God unto salvation **(Romans 1:16).** And when we, as evangelists, stand to preach, we are not offering an alternative—we are delivering the only hope humanity has.

What Is the Gospel?
(1 Corinthians 15:1–4)

The apostle Paul, writing with urgency and clarity, lays out the Gospel in unmistakable terms:

"Let me now remind you, dear brothers and sisters, of the Good News I preached to you before… It is this Good News that saves you… I passed on to you what was most important and what had also been passed on to me. Christ died for our sins, just as the Scriptures said. He was buried, and He was raised from the dead on the third day, just as the Scriptures said."
(1 Corinthians 15:1–4, NLT)

Let's break it down:

- Christ died for our sins – Not for surface struggles, not for generational dysfunctions, but for the sin that separated us from God. The cross was not symbolic—it was violent redemption. The innocent Lamb was slaughtered in our place.

- He was buried – Jesus truly died. He didn't faint or slip into a coma. He entered the grave, bearing our guilt and shame, and fulfilled the penalty of sin in full.

- He rose again – This is not myth or metaphor. It is a historical fact, witnessed by hundreds. He conquered death, disarmed hell, and emerged victorious. The resurrection wasn't the end—it was the beginning of new creation for all who believe.

This is the Gospel. Not self-improvement. Not moral adjustment. Not positive energy. The Gospel is the announcement that Jesus has done what we never could: He satisfied the wrath of God and made a way back home.

And if we, as evangelists, do not preach this, then what we preach cannot save.

Jesus: Savior, Lord, and Coming King

Too many have accepted a half-gospel—a message that says, "Come to Jesus and life will improve." But Jesus didn't come to make our old life better. He came to put it to death and give us a new one.

- Jesus is Savior – He rescues us from sin's penalty and power. He doesn't just comfort the sinner—He cleanses them. He doesn't just offer a hand—He offers a heart transplant. He saves us from something (hell) and to something (relationship with the Father). He came to seek and to save the lost (Luke 19:10), and His arm is still reaching.

- Jesus is Lord – Salvation is not an escape hatch—it is an entrance into the Kingdom. We don't just receive mercy; we come under divine rule. "Jesus is Lord" is not a religious phrase—it is a declaration of surrender. His Word becomes our authority. His will becomes our pursuit. He saves us, and then He leads us.

- Jesus is the Coming King – The Gospel does not end at the cross or even the resurrection. It ends in glory. Christ is returning—not in weakness, but in fire. Not as a baby in a manger, but as a Judge on a throne. His return is not optional doctrine—it is the final chapter. It gives the Gospel its urgency. It fuels the mission of every evangelist. We preach now because He is coming soon.

So when you preach Jesus, preach all of Him. Preach the Lamb and the Lion. Preach the mercy and the majesty. Preach the cross and the crown.

Repentance, Faith, and the Power of Grace

The Gospel demands more than agreement—it demands a response. This is not news to analyze; it is a summons to obey.

- Repentance – This is not mere emotion or religious regret. It is a full turning of the heart, mind, and life. It is confession, yes—but it is also abandonment of sin. Jesus didn't say, **"Try your best." He said, "Repent, for the Kingdom of Heaven is at hand." (Matthew 4:17)**. Repentance is not legalism—it is the highway to freedom. Without it, there is no transformation. And we must not edit it out of the message.

- Faith – Faith is more than belief—it is trust. It is the open hand of the soul, receiving grace. It believes the cross was personal, the resurrection was literal, and the promises of God are eternal. Faith doesn't wait for feelings—it clings to the truth. And it is through faith that we are justified and born again.

- Grace – This is not permission to sin—it is the power to overcome it. Grace doesn't just pardon—it trains, transforms, and empowers. As Paul told Titus:

"The grace of God... teaches us to say 'No' to ungodliness..." (Titus 2:11–12).

True grace strengthens our yes to God and our no to the flesh. It is not soft—it is supernatural.

Every time you share the Gospel, call for this response: Repent. Believe. Surrender. Because only then can the soul be born from above and sealed for eternity.

Preach the Real Gospel

Evangelist, do not preach a diluted Gospel. Don't preach cultural Christianity. Don't preach self-help with a Jesus sticker. Don't preach comfort when the message is crucifixion. Preach the Gospel of power—the cross that confronts, the tomb that testifies, and the King who is coming.

Preach it with tears. Preach it with urgency. Preach it to the crowd and to the one. And never assume they already know.

Every soul is on a collision course with eternity. And you carry the message that can reroute their destiny.

The Gospel is not something we outgrow. It is not something we tweak. It is not something we tame. It is the eternal message that split time in half, defeated hell, and opened heaven.

So let it burn in your bones. Let it fuel your mission. And let it be the message you carry until your final breath.

Because this Gospel—it's worth dying for.

And even more—it's worth living for.

Chapter 5
Preparation for Evangelism

Fueling the Fire Before You Go

Before a soldier enters battle, he trains and arms himself. Before a farmer plants, he plows and prepares the ground. Before an evangelist opens their mouth to preach the Gospel, they must be prepared—not just with knowledge, but with fire, conviction, and spiritual authority.

Evangelism is not a hobby. It is not a side project. It is a divine assignment. And spiritual assignments require spiritual preparation.

Without preparation, you may have passion—but no power. You may inspire people—but not transform them. You may draw a crowd—but not make disciples. There is a difference between stirring emotion and releasing anointing. The evangelist must be ready in spirit, not just ready in speech.

Prayer, Fasting, and Being Led by the Spirit

Evangelism does not begin with a microphone. It begins with your knees on the floor.

The public ministry of power must be preceded by private intimacy with God. Before Peter thundered at Pentecost, he was hidden in a prayer meeting. Before Paul turned cities upside down, he fasted, prayed, and heard from the Lord. Even Jesus, the Son of God, rose early to commune with the Father. If you don't prioritize the secret place, you'll eventually have nothing to offer in the public place.

Prayer isn't a ritual—it's where fire is born. You don't just inform God—you receive from Him. His burden becomes yours. His heart becomes yours. His strategy becomes yours. Prayer aligns the evangelist with Heaven's timetable. You'll know where to go, when to speak, and who to reach—because you've listened before you've acted.

Fasting adds weight to your preparation. It silences the flesh and tunes your spirit. It's not about suffering to prove something to God—it's about making room. Fasting declares, "I want You more than food. I want souls more than comfort. I want power more than popularity." The flesh will never lead you into revival—but fasting crucifies the flesh and clears the way for the Spirit.

Jesus said, **"Some kinds only come out by prayer and fasting" (Mark 9:29, NKJV).** There are regions that won't break open without a consecrated messenger. There are moments that demand more than enthusiasm—they demand a consecrated life. Fasting doesn't just prepare the atmosphere—it prepares you.

Then comes being led by the Spirit. Evangelism isn't just about speaking—it's about moving with God. Philip didn't choose the desert road—he was sent there **(Acts 8:26).** Paul didn't go everywhere he wanted—he was redirected by the Holy Spirit **(Acts 16:6–10).** The evangelist must never be driven by trends, doors, or human reasoning. You must be Spirit-led—because the Spirit knows where the hungry are.

Don't mistake movement for mission. Just because you're busy doesn't mean you're effective. The Holy Spirit has divine appointments waiting—but only the prepared, prayerful, and discerning will find them.

Understanding Your Spiritual Authority

When you preach the Gospel, you're not merely addressing minds—you're confronting principalities. The god of this world blinds minds **(2 Corinthians 4:4)**, sin enslaves hearts, and demons resist the advance of truth. That means evangelism is warfare.

You must know your authority. You are not speaking in your own name—you are coming in the name of the King. Jesus said:

"I have given you authority over all the power of the enemy…" (Luke 10:19 NLT)

Authority is not volume—it's spiritual rank. It's not based on feelings or experience—it's based on your position in Christ. You have been seated with Christ in heavenly places **(Ephesians 2:6).** You carry the name above every name. When you speak the truth, the devil trembles—not because of who you are, but because of who backs you.

But this authority must be understood and walked in. You must know:

- That you've been cleansed by the blood.

- That you've been filled with the Spirit.

- That you've been commissioned by Christ Himself.

When you walk in spiritual authority, you don't shrink back. You speak with conviction. You pray with fire. You command with faith. You bind, loose, and stand. The evangelist is not a timid talker—they are an authorized representative of Heaven, proclaiming the end of Satan's rule and the arrival of God's Kingdom.

Don't enter the harvest field unsure of your identity. The enemy will always attack your confidence. But when you know who you are and whose you are, you walk into spiritual battlegrounds with boldness.

Studying Scripture to Sharpen Your Sword

The evangelist's weapon is not charisma—it's truth. The Gospel is not a product to be sold—it is a sword to be wielded. And that sword is Scripture.

If you don't know the Word, you are not prepared. If you don't study the Word, you are not safe. The evangelist must be immersed in truth—saturated, anchored, and equipped.

Paul's charge to Timothy still stands:

"Preach the word... Be prepared, whether the time is favorable or not." (2 Timothy 4:2 NLT)

That means whether the crowd is hungry or hostile, you are ready. Whether the conversation is planned or spontaneous, you are sharp. Whether you're in a pulpit, a café, or a jail cell—you have the Word hidden in your heart and ready on your lips.

Practical preparation includes:

- Memorizing key verses **(John 3:16, Romans 3:23, Romans 6:23, Ephesians 2:8–9, etc.)**

- Studying the Gospel presentations in **Acts (Acts 2, 3, 8, 10, 13, 17)**

- Understanding how to lead someone in repentance, faith, and surrender

- Being able to answer objections with Scripture, not just opinion

- Walking through salvation conversations with clarity and love

Don't build your ministry on borrowed revelation. Get your own. Let the Word pierce you before you preach it. Let it form your theology, your tone, your urgency. When the Word lives in you, the Spirit can draw it out in divine moments.

It is not emotion that saves. It is truth—empowered by the Spirit, rooted in Christ, and spoken through the prepared heart of a yielded evangelist.

The Furnace Before the Fire

Before you preach, prepare. Burn in secret before you blaze in public. Let prayer be your preparation, fasting be your consecration, the Spirit be your direction, and the Word be your sword. Don't just be passionate—be dangerous to darkness.

You are not going to entertain—you are going to rescue. You are not going to impress—you are going to deliver the Word of life. And that requires more than gifting. It requires depth.

So train like a soldier. Study like a scholar. Pray like a prophet. And fast like a warrior. Because the souls waiting on the other side of your obedience are worth the cost.

Chapter 6
Power Evangelism

Demonstrating the Gospel With Fire and Authority

The Gospel is not only to be heard—it is to be seen. The Kingdom of God does not advance by persuasive words alone, but by the demonstration of the Spirit and power **(1 Corinthians 2:4)**. Jesus didn't just teach the truth—He manifested it. He healed the sick, cast out demons, multiplied food, raised the dead, and spoke words that shook the natural and spiritual realms alike.

When Jesus commissioned His disciples, He did not send them out with only theology—He sent them with power. That same power that flowed through Him now flows through those who believe. Evangelism without power is like a lamp without oil. But when the Word is preached with authority, and the Spirit is present to confirm it—everything changes.

This is Power Evangelism. Not a fad. Not a movement. Not reserved for "charismatics." It is the biblical model of Gospel proclamation—bold speech backed by divine intervention. When we recover this, we don't just preach the Kingdom—we demonstrate it.

Signs, Wonders, and Miracles as Confirmation

Jesus didn't just proclaim the Kingdom—He proved it.

> "And the disciples went everywhere and preached, and the Lord worked through them, confirming what they said by many miraculous signs."

(Mark 16:20, NLT)

Miracles do not replace the Gospel—but they confirm it. They validate the messenger, arrest the attention of the lost, and break through spiritual resistance.

In **Acts 8**, Philip enters Samaria—not with a strategy, but with power:

> **"Crowds listened intently to Philip because they were eager to hear his message and see the miraculous signs he did... Many evil spirits were cast out... and many who had been paralyzed or lame were healed. So there was great joy in that city."**

(Acts 8:6–8, NLT)

The supernatural didn't compete with the message—it amplified it. Philip didn't build a stage—he brought the Kingdom. He didn't market a ministry—he walked in fire.

This is not just biblical history—it's our apostolic inheritance.

> **"My message and my preaching were not with wise and persuasive words, but with a demonstration of the Spirit's power."**

(1 Corinthians 2:4, NIV)

Evangelists must recover this. People may resist your logic—but they cannot deny the supernatural. Power evangelism silences intellectual arrogance, awakens spiritual hunger, and makes Jesus real in a way that no argument can.

Miracles don't save—but they do prepare the heart for salvation.

Healing the Sick, Casting Out Demons, Prophetic Encounters

Jesus said:

"Heal the sick, raise the dead, cleanse those who have leprosy, drive out demons. Freely you have received; freely give."
(Matthew 10:8, NIV)

That wasn't just for the twelve. It was the standard of Kingdom ministry.

Heal the Sick

Healing displays God's compassion and proves His authority. It reveals that the curse has been broken and the Kingdom is at hand. Whether on a street corner or in a stadium, when the sick are healed, eyes open and hearts listen.

- Jesus healed as a sign of His Lordship **(Luke 5:24).**

- The apostles healed in His name **(Acts 3:6–8).**

- And believers today are still called to lay hands on the sick (Mark 16:18).

Let healing flow—not as a spectacle, but as a demonstration of mercy.

Cast Out Demons

Deliverance is not a fringe ministry—it is central to Gospel work.

- Jesus cast out demons in synagogues, streets, and private homes.

- The early Church did the same—with boldness and authority.

- Wherever the Gospel is truly preached, darkness is confronted.

Evangelists must not fear this. When the anointing is strong, demons will manifest. Don't panic. Don't negotiate. Command them to leave. You carry the authority of Christ. Use it.

Deliverance shows that the cross didn't just forgive sin—it crushed Satan.

Release Prophetic Words

When Jesus read the woman at the well's mail, her heart was unlocked. Prophetic evangelism is powerful because it proves God sees, knows, and loves the individual.

- A word of knowledge can reveal hidden pain.

- A prophetic word can unlock destiny.

- A Spirit-led word can soften even the hardest skeptic.

Desire spiritual gifts. Ask the Lord to speak through you—not for your sake, but for theirs.

"Eagerly desire the gifts of the Spirit, especially prophecy." (1 Corinthians 14:1, NIV)

The prophetic is not fortune-telling—it is the voice of God reaching into the heart of a soul bound in darkness.

Walking in Boldness Through the Holy Spirit

Everything we've described—healing, deliverance, prophetic encounters—flows from one Person: the Holy Spirit.

Jesus didn't let His disciples begin their mission until they were filled.

"But you will receive power when the Holy Spirit comes upon you. And you will be my witnesses..."
(Acts 1:8, NLT)

Power precedes proclamation. Fire precedes fruit. Pentecost must come before public ministry.

You may have passion—but without the Holy Spirit, you lack power. Boldness is not human confidence—it is Spirit-infused courage. Peter, the denier, became Peter, the preacher—because he was filled with the Holy Spirit. When the Spirit fills you:

- Fear breaks.

- Courage rises.

- Obedience flows.

- And the atmosphere shifts.

Holy Spirit boldness isn't about volume. It's about clarity and courage in the face of fear, rejection, and resistance.

The same Spirit who hovered over the waters in Genesis, the same Spirit who raised Jesus from the dead, the same Spirit who shook the upper room—dwells in you. You are not alone when you preach. You are carried.

Power Evangelism: Not Optional, But Biblical

We must return to this standard. Not every evangelist will see miracles every day—but every evangelist should expect the supernatural to follow them.

Jesus said:

"These signs will accompany those who believe…"
(Mark 16:17, NLT)

Not "might." Not "sometimes." But will. The signs follow the believing believer—not the skeptical speaker.

- Don't just give information—bring impartation.

- Don't just quote verses—demonstrate victory.

- Don't just explain Jesus—reveal Him through power.

The world has heard enough words. It's time they see the Gospel in action.

Let Power Return

The Gospel is not entertainment—it is an invasion. When you preach, don't be content with explanation. Press in for demonstration. Seek God for fire. Obey the promptings of the Spirit. Stretch your hand toward the sick. Command demons to flee. Speak prophetically into dry bones. And let the Gospel live.

You were never called to be a silent messenger. You are a burning torch. You are a vessel of glory. You are the one who carries both Word and wonder.

Preach Christ—and let power follow.

Chapter 7
One-on-One
Soul-Winning

The Power of the Personal Gospel

Mass crusades, open-air preaching, and citywide revivals have their place. They shake regions, mobilize churches, and reap massive harvests. But Heaven does not rejoice over crowds—it rejoices over the one. Jesus said, **"There is joy in the presence of the angels of God over one sinner that repenteth." (Luke 15:10, KJV)**

Some of the most eternal, powerful moments in evangelism do not happen in stadiums or from platforms. They happen in whispered conversations across tables. In tear-filled moments at bus stops. In spontaneous prayers beside hospital beds. In vulnerable exchanges in locker rooms, break rooms, and parking lots. These are the sacred spaces of one-on-one soul-winning—where eternity invades the ordinary.

Jesus modeled this. Yes, He preached to multitudes—but He also stopped for the one. He saw Zacchaeus in a tree and called him down. He waited at a well for a woman carrying shame. He walked into a tax booth and rewrote Levi's future. He turned aside in a crowd to speak to a woman bleeding with pain. These weren't interruptions—they were divine appointments. And when we live in step with the Spirit, we will find that our greatest Gospel opportunities often look like "ordinary moments."

Evangelists must not underestimate this sacred form of outreach. It is not less powerful than public ministry. In many ways, it is more fruitful, more lasting, and more transformative. One-on-one soul-winning is not event-based—it is life-based. It's relational. It's intentional. And it makes room not just for decisions, but for discipleship.

Evangelism Begins with Seeing

Before you ever speak, you must see. One-on-one evangelism starts with spiritual awareness.

Too many believers walk past people every day and never see them. Our eyes are filled with schedules, distractions, and self-focus. But evangelists must train their spiritual sight. They must walk slowly through the crowds. They must be attentive to tears, heaviness, isolation, fear, and open doors.

Jesus was always watching. When others saw the Samaritan woman as a scandal, He saw a seeker. When others avoided the leper, He touched him. When others condemned the woman caught in adultery, He forgave her. When the crowd saw a thief on a cross, Jesus saw a man one breath away from glory.

That kind of vision comes from intimacy with the Holy Spirit. He will show you the one that others ignore. And when you see them—not as a statistic, but as a son or daughter—it changes everything. You won't preach at them. You'll reach for them.

How to Engage in One-on-One Witnessing

This is not a script. It's a posture. And it starts with love and sensitivity to the Holy Spirit.

1. Start with Relationship or Respect

DO THE WORK OF AN EVANGELIST

Every soul matters. Whether it's a friend you've known for years or a stranger you meet in passing, approach them with dignity.

- Be kind. Be real. Smile.

- Don't rush into a sermon—be present.

- If it's someone you know, invest in the relationship.

- If it's someone you just met, let your tone and body language speak grace.

Sometimes the Spirit will prompt you to speak immediately. Other times, He will have you plant seeds. Either way—be sensitive, not pushy.

2. Discern the Openness

The Spirit will show you who is ripe for harvest. Some people will open up through casual conversation. Others will be in crisis. Some are spiritually curious. Others are silently desperate.

Ask simple Spirit-led questions:

- "Can I pray for you?"

- "Have you ever experienced the love of God?"

- "Do you know Jesus personally?"

- "If today was your last day, are you ready to meet God?"

These are not manipulations. They are invitations. You are not pressuring—you're fishing.

3. Tell Your Story

Paul shared his testimony often. He didn't always start with doctrine—he started with his encounter. Your story carries power. It reveals Jesus in you.

Tell people:

- Who you were before Christ.

- How He met you.

- What He has changed.

Keep it honest. Keep it Jesus-focused. Don't glorify the sin—glorify the Savior.

People may argue theology, but they cannot argue with your transformation. When you are vulnerable, they will open up. And your story will become a bridge to the cross.

4. Share the Gospel Clearly

Don't get distracted by side conversations. Bring it back to Jesus.

- God created us for relationship.

- Sin broke that relationship.

- Jesus came, lived without sin, died in our place, and rose again.

- Through repentance and faith, we are restored to God.

"For all have sinned, and come short of the glory of God." (Romans 3:23)

"But God commendeth his love toward us, in that, while we were yet sinners, Christ died for us." (Romans 5:8)

"That if thou shalt confess with thy mouth the Lord Jesus, and shalt believe in thine heart that God hath raised him from the dead, thou shalt be saved." (Romans 10:9)

Be clear. Be bold. Ask for a response:

"Would you like to surrender your life to Jesus right now?"

Don't fear the silence. Don't back away. Let the Holy Spirit do the work. Be ready to lead them into the Kingdom.

5. Lead Them in Sincere Surrender

If they say yes—slow down. Don't make it mechanical. Make it meaningful.

Lead them in repentance and faith. Let them confess Jesus from the heart. Guide them if needed:

"Jesus, I believe You died for me and rose again. I turn from my sin and surrender to You. Be my Lord and Savior. Wash me, fill me, and make me Yours. Amen."

Let the tears fall. Let the Spirit move. Make it sacred. Don't rush to the next thing. Heaven is rejoicing.

6. Follow Up and Walk With Them

Jesus didn't say "make converts"—He said, "make disciples."

- Get their number.

- Help them get a Bible.

- Invite them to church.

- Walk with them.

Text them. Pray with them. Study Scripture together. One-on-one soul-winning often becomes one-on-one discipling. That's how fruit remains.

"I have chosen you, and ordained you, that ye should go and bring forth fruit, and that your fruit should remain..." (John 15:16)

Soul-Winning Is a Lifestyle

This is not something you schedule—this is something you live.

Be ready in line at the store. Be alert at the gas pump. Be available at the gym. Soul-winning isn't about convenience—it's about eternity. Keep Gospel tracts in your pocket, testimonies in your mouth, and fire in your heart.

Jesus said:

"The Son of man is come to seek and to save that which was lost." (Luke 19:10)

If that's why He came, then that's why you go.

The Power of One

Never underestimate the impact of one soul. One life transformed can spark revival. One yes to Jesus can change a family line. One act of obedience can birth eternal fruit.

You may not remember the full conversation. But Heaven does. You may never see the ripple effect. But eternity will.

You are not too busy to stop. You are not too ordinary to be used. You are not too small to make a Kingdom impact. When you stop for the one, Jesus walks with you.

So evangelist—slow down. Watch. Listen. Speak. Pray. Love.

This is the Gospel up close. This is the Kingdom in motion.

This is the sacred power of one-on-one soul-winning.

Chapter 8
Street and Public Evangelism

Bringing the Gospel Where the People Are

The Gospel was never meant to be confined to buildings. It was born on the streets—announced in the open, preached in marketplaces, cried aloud in wildernesses, and shouted from prison cells. Jesus did not isolate Himself behind temple walls. He walked among the people. He preached in fields, boats, hillsides, and cities. He moved with compassion and power where the broken were.

The early Church didn't wait for perfect venues or polished pulpits. They carried the Gospel into the streets. And we must do the same. Public evangelism is not outdated—it is desperately needed. In a time of moral confusion, cultural chaos, and spiritual darkness, the Church must not retreat. We must rise and reclaim the streets with truth, love, and holy fire.

This chapter is a summons—to leave the comfort zone, step into the open, and lift up the name of Jesus without apology. We must preach in city centers, street corners, festivals, parks, campuses, beaches, and marketplaces. If the devil is loud in public, the Church must be louder with righteousness. One soul at a time. One street at a time.

The Biblical Precedent for Open-Air Preaching

Open-air preaching is not a modern idea—it is an ancient pattern of divine movement.

- Jesus preached outdoors continually. The Sermon on the Mount **(Matthew 5–7)** was delivered on a hillside. He preached in boats **(Luke 5:3)**, along roads, in homes, and beside wells. He healed in public, wept in public, and declared the Kingdom where the crowds were—not just inside the synagogues.

- John the Baptist stood in the wilderness and cried out, **"Repent ye: for the kingdom of heaven is at hand" (Matthew 3:2)**. He had no building, no band, no website—just a burning word and a river.

- Peter stood in the streets of Jerusalem during Pentecost and boldly declared that Jesus was both Lord and Christ. **"Then they that gladly received his word were baptized: and the same day there were added unto them about three thousand souls." (Acts 2:41)**

- Paul preached in synagogues and in the marketplaces **(Acts 17:17)**. He debated with philosophers on Mars Hill **(Acts 17:22–31)**. He evangelized in homes, cities, and courts, never waiting for the "ideal setting." His method was simple: Where there are people, there must be preaching.

God has always anointed bold public proclamation. He doesn't hide His message behind walls—He announces it with power. **"Cry aloud, spare not, lift up thy voice like a trumpet…" (Isaiah 58:1)**

When Spirit-filled believers take the Gospel into the streets, heaven touches earth and the atmosphere shifts.

How to Prepare for Street and Public Evangelism
1. Pray with Purpose and Authority

Before you preach, pray. Prayer is not a ritual—it is alignment. Before Jesus ministered to multitudes, He withdrew to pray **(Mark 1:35)**. He was not performing spiritual gymnastics—He was staying connected to the Father.

Pray with the Word. Pray with faith. And pray with expectation. Ask the Lord to:

- Soften the hearts of the people you'll encounter.

- Direct your steps to the right place at the right time.

- Fill you with boldness, compassion, and clarity.

- Silence distractions and release supernatural peace.

You don't have to "take territory"—you already carry authority in Christ. The Gospel itself is the power of God unto salvation **(Romans 1:16)**. The goal is not hype—but Holy Spirit anointing.

2. Go With Others When Possible

Jesus sent His disciples out two by two **(Mark 6:7)**. Partnership increases impact.

Go in teams for:

- Mutual encouragement

- Safety

- Expanded ministry (one can preach, another can pray, another can engage personally)

Some may be loud. Some may be quiet. Some may hold signs. Some may sing or worship. Everyone has a role—but Christ must remain the center.

3. Know Your Message—Preach Christ with Clarity

Street evangelism demands focus. There is no time for theological debates or controversial side topics. Preach the Gospel. Preach the cross. Preach Jesus crucified, buried, risen, and returning.

"For I determined not to know any thing among you, save Jesus Christ, and him crucified."

(1 Corinthians 2:2)

Tell people:

- Sin separates, but Christ reconciles.

- Jesus is the only way to the Father **(John 14:6).**

- Repentance and faith bring salvation.

- Heaven is real. So is Hell. But mercy is available now.

You don't need to impress people. You need to pierce them with truth—lovingly, boldly, and biblically.

4. Use What God Has Given You

You don't need a stage to preach. Use your gifts and creativity:

- Guitar and worship songs

- Testimonies and spoken word

- Sketchboards or visuals

- Prayer stations

- Free water bottles or tracts with Scripture

- Personal conversations or prophetic evangelism

Let your tools support the Gospel—not overshadow it. Gimmicks fade. The Word remains.

5. Stay Spirit-Led, Not Script-Driven

Have a plan—but hold it loosely. The Holy Spirit might shift your message mid-sentence. Be interruptible.

He may:

- Highlight a specific person.

- Stir a word of knowledge or prophetic insight.

- Prompt you to change locations or approaches.

Public evangelism is not performance—it is partnership with the Spirit of God.

"For as many as are led by the Spirit of God, they are the sons of God."
(Romans 8:14)

Dealing with Opposition, Mockery, and Fear

You will face resistance. Jesus said:

"And ye shall be hated of all men for my name's sake..."
(Matthew 10:22)

Some will scoff. Some will argue. Some may mock or curse you. But remember:

- You're not responsible for results. You're responsible for obedience.

- The message offends because it confronts sin. But it also offers hope.

- You are not alone. Heaven backs you.

Paul said:

"For I am not ashamed of the gospel of Christ: for it is the power of God unto salvation to every one that believeth…"

(Romans 1:16)

Do not argue with mockers. Do not shrink back from fear. Speak truth in love. Let your demeanor be humble, but let your words carry weight.

The apostles were beaten, imprisoned, and threatened. Yet they declared:

"We cannot but speak the things which we have seen and heard."

(Acts 4:20)

If you're hated for His name, you're in good company. Keep preaching.

Strategic Locations and Spirit-Led Timing

Let God lead your feet and guide your time. Jesus never randomly wandered—He was always sent.

Effective public locations include:

- City squares and street corners

- Parks, campuses, beaches, and fairs

- Transit hubs—bus stops, train stations, airports

- Outside government buildings or clinics

- Areas known for homelessness, addiction, or spiritual oppression

DO THE WORK OF AN EVANGELIST

The where and when matters. Ask the Lord:
- Where is the greatest need?
- Where are the hungry hearts?
- When is the best moment for harvest?

Sometimes it's not a loud crowd but a quiet moment with a single person that changes a destiny.

Final Charge: Go Where They Are

The Church must not wait for people to come—we must go to them. Jesus said:

"Go out into the highways and hedges, and compel them to come in, that my house may be filled."
(Luke 14:23)

The streets are crying. The cities are groaning. The world is searching.

Evangelist, arise. Take your voice, your Bible, your fire—and go where the people are. Don't fear the noise. Don't wait for comfort. Preach in season and out of season. Preach Christ crucified, risen, and returning.

The same Holy Spirit who filled Peter on Pentecost is ready to fill you now.

Lift up your voice. Sound the alarm. Let the Gospel echo again in the streets.

Chapter 9
Evangelism in the Local Church

Let the Church Burn for the Harvest

The Church was never called to be a spectator gathering. It is Heaven's war room and Jesus' body on the earth. Jesus did not say, "Wait for the lost to find their way in." He said, **"Go ye into all the world, and preach the gospel to every creature." (Mark 16:15)**

That commission was not given only to individual believers. It was a charge to the Church as a whole. Every local church—large or small, rural or urban, traditional or modern—is meant to be a soul-winning center, a sending station, and a beacon of truth in the middle of a lost world.

A church that does not evangelize is a church that has lost its pulse. A church that does not carry the burden of the lost is a church that has drifted from the heart of God. The Gospel that is not preached will be forgotten. The Gospel that is not proclaimed will be assumed. And a Gospel that is assumed will soon be lost.

Evangelism must not be a program or a quarterly initiative. It must become the culture—woven into the prayers, preaching, worship, structure, and identity of the church.

If the Church is truly the body of Christ, then it must also carry the heartbeat of Christ—**"to seek and to save that which was lost." (Luke 19:10)**

Equipping the Saints to Evangelize

The role of church leadership is not to do all the ministry—it is to equip the saints for it.

"And he gave some, apostles; and some, prophets; and some, evangelists; and some, pastors and teachers; for the perfecting of the saints, for the work of the ministry...". (Ephesians 4:11–12)

That includes equipping for evangelism.

Every member of the body—young or old, new or seasoned—is a potential soul-winner. The role of pastors and leaders is to:

- Equip the church to share their testimony with boldness.

- Teach them to clearly explain the Gospel.

- Train them to lead others to Christ both in and outside the building.

- Empower them to minister with both compassion and conviction.

Too often, we delegate evangelism to the evangelist, while God has filled the pews with people carrying the Gospel inside of them. What if every believer knew how to lead someone to Christ? What if every usher, worshipper, teacher, and intercessor carried a burden for souls?

Equip your people. Preach it. Model it. Hold evangelism training regularly. Teach the Romans Road. Role-play Gospel conversations. Create moments for outreach activation and prayer for boldness.

Evangelism must not be outsourced. It must be activated in the house.

Sunday Services Must Be Evangelistic

The Sunday gathering is more than a family reunion. It is also a rescue mission. Each service is an opportunity for souls to encounter the truth, feel conviction, and receive salvation.

"Preach the word; be instant in season, out of season; reprove, rebuke, exhort with all longsuffering and doctrine." (2 Timothy 4:2)

We must not preach only for the edification of the saved—we must preach for the salvation of the lost.

Every Sunday:

- Assume someone is in the room who is far from God.

- Assume someone has never heard the Gospel clearly.

- Assume someone walked in hoping this is their last chance.

That means the Gospel must be clear in every message. Deep truth should not exclude simple salvation. Do not dilute the message—but make it accessible. Preach repentance. Preach the cross. Preach the blood. Preach Jesus. And then give space for response.

Don't rush altar calls. Don't move past conviction. Train your altar workers to discern brokenness, pray with fire, and minister with wisdom. Every response matters. One life turning to Christ is worth pausing the whole service.

Let worship teams sing with eternity in mind. Let greeters welcome with love. Let intercessors cover the room in prayer. Let every part of the Sunday service reflect a love for the lost, not just the found.

Outreach Must Be Intentional and Ongoing

Evangelism that stays inside the four walls is incomplete.

The Gospel must be taken outside—into streets, schools, shelters, hospitals, apartment complexes, prisons, and public places. Jesus said:
"Go ye into all the world..." (Mark 16:15)
Not "wait until they come in." Go.
Outreach must be:

- Consistent – not once a year, but a regular rhythm.

- Strategic – led by the Spirit, not just tradition.

- Inclusive – engaging every age, background, and gifting.

Ideas include:

- Weekly or monthly street ministry.

- Prayer walks in neighborhoods and campuses.

- Door-to-door Gospel and invitation.

- Evangelistic events (barbecues, concerts, sports nights).

- Partnerships with schools, recovery homes, and local outreach groups.

- Follow-up ministries to care for new believers from the community.

Make it easy for people to join. Provide clear training. Share testimonies. Celebrate fruit. Let evangelism be normalized—not rare, not strange, but central to the life of the church.

Build a Culture of Invitation

Inviting someone to church is simple—but powerful. Andrew brought Peter to Jesus. The woman at the well told her village. The man set free from demons went back to Decapolis.

Evangelism starts with an invitation.

Train your people to:

- Invite friends, neighbors, and coworkers.

- Share their testimony online.

- Carry invite cards in their pockets.

- Pray over empty chairs and ask God to fill them.

Encourage invitations to:
- Sunday services

- Special events and revivals

- Small groups and Bible studies

- Youth nights, men's and women's gatherings

Create services that are friendly to the unchurched, without compromising truth. Make on-ramps simple, accessible, and full of grace. When every member of the church becomes a bridge, the community will come.

Let Evangelism Shape Your Culture

Evangelism must not be a department. It must be our DNA.

Let it touch everything:

- Prayer – intercede for the lost by name.

- Preaching – include altar calls often, not rarely.

- Worship – sing songs of harvest, redemption, and power.

- Testimonies – let new believers share from the mic.

- Budget – invest in outreach, Bibles, tracts, and training.

- Children and Youth – train them to win souls from an early age.

- Follow-up – make disciples, not just converts.

Let greeters be missionaries at the door. Let children's workers plant seeds of salvation. Let pastors cry over the altar again. Let evangelists be given space and celebration in the house.

A church that evangelizes is a church alive. It grows. It vibrates with vision. It shakes with tears and testimonies. It mirrors the Savior who left the 99 to go after the one.

Evangelism is not one program among many. It is the pulse of a church on fire.

The Whole Church, The Whole Gospel, For the Whole World

Pastor, leader, intercessor, usher—you are part of the mission. Jesus said:

"Follow me, and I will make you fishers of men."
(Matthew 4:19)

To follow Jesus is to fish. A church that follows Jesus must reach. Let your church be known:

- Not just for powerful worship—but for powerful witness.

- Not just for great sermons—but for great salvations.

- Not just for big crowds—but for changed lives.

- For baptisms, for tears of repentance, for new birth, for the sound of Heaven rejoicing.

This is the heart of revival. This is the dream of God.
Let your church burn for the harvest.

Chapter 10
Digital Evangelism

Preaching Christ in the Digital Public Square

We are living in the most connected generation in human history. A single voice can now be heard across nations in seconds. While the early Church journeyed by foot, boat, and beast to carry the Gospel, today we have the power to proclaim Christ to millions with a device in our hand.

This is not coincidence—it is divine opportunity.

The internet is not just technology—it is a territory. And the Church must stop surrendering it to darkness. If the world is online, the Church must be on mission there. Evangelism is not confined to the pulpit—it is called to the platforms. We are not waiting for people to walk into buildings—we are bringing the message to them, wherever they are, including their phones, laptops, and earbuds.

This is not about trendiness—it's about truth going forth with power. We are not promoting personalities. We are proclaiming the Gospel of Jesus Christ.

Why Digital Evangelism Matters

The online world is where people now live. With over 5 billion internet users and countless hours spent on social media, streaming, and searching—it has become one of the largest unreached mission fields.

Digital evangelism matters because it allows us to:
- Reach beyond the walls of our churches and cities.
- Connect with people in hostile nations where missionaries cannot enter.
- Interrupt darkness with light in the same feed where sin is celebrated.
- Minister to the broken where they are already searching for answers.
- Multiply the impact of one voice, one message, one testimony.

Paul used parchment and ink. Luther used the printing press. Today, we use phones and cameras. The tools change, but the commission does not.

"So then faith cometh by hearing, and hearing by the word of God."
(Romans 10:17)

The Word must be heard. And in this generation, it must be heard online.

Using Social Media with Purpose and Power

Social media is a tool. It can distract—or it can disciple. It can destroy—or it can deliver. The difference lies in who uses it—and how.

1. Be Real, Not Religious

People are not looking for staged religion—they're looking for authentic transformation. You don't need to be polished. You need to be genuine. Let your posts, videos, and captions reflect who you are in Christ. Share your journey. Talk about your encounters with God. Let them see real faith in a real world.

Testify. Declare what Jesus did. Don't fake perfection. Tell the truth—and let grace shine.

2. Share the Gospel Boldly and Clearly

If your platform belongs to Jesus, then use it to preach Him.

Post Scriptures. Share the cross. Call for repentance. Declare His love. Don't only post encouragement—post the Gospel. Don't just offer comfort—offer conversion.

- Create short reels explaining salvation.

- Share posts that invite people to respond to Christ.

- Include a call to action: "DM me if you want prayer," or "Comment 'Jesus' if you want to surrender your life."

You don't need a perfect setup. You need a clear message and a burning heart.

"For I determined not to know any thing among you, save Jesus Christ, and him crucified."

(1 Corinthians 2:2)

3. Create Engaging, Shareable Content

The world scrolls quickly—make the Gospel stand out.

- Use strong visuals and captions that point to truth.

- Film short testimonies or teachings.

- Share powerful Scriptures with real-life application.

- Record voice notes with prophetic encouragement.

- Start a blog, write devotionals, or host live Q&As.

You don't need a marketing degree. You need clarity, truth, and anointing.

Let your creativity be sanctified. Let your design glorify Christ. Don't post for applause—post to provoke hearts.

4. Respond and Minister in the DMs

Ministry is still relational—even online. Don't just post and disappear.

- Respond to comments.

- Answer questions with truth and grace.

- Follow up with those who reach out.

- Lead people in prayers of salvation in private messages.

- Send voice notes, Scriptures, and encouragement.

Every digital connection can become a divine encounter. Treat them as holy moments.

5. Be Consistent and Led by the Spirit

Don't wait until your platform is big. Start now. If you reach one, it was worth it.

Post consistently. Let your presence online be known as one who carries the Gospel. Ask the Holy Spirit what to share, when to speak, and how to say it. Be bold. Be obedient.

"What I tell you in darkness, that speak ye in light: and what ye hear in the ear, that preach ye upon the housetops."

(Matthew 10:27)

In this generation, the housetops are digital.

Podcasting, Livestreams, and Video Evangelism

If you feel called to teach or testify regularly—consider expanding into deeper formats:

- Start a podcast – Teach Scripture, interview believers, answer spiritual questions.

- Go live – Pray for healing, share a word from God, respond to comments.

- Launch a YouTube channel – Create teaching series, testimony features, or prophetic warnings.

Many will scroll past a church building—but click on a video in secret. Many are not ready to walk through the doors—but they are listening.

Reach them. Speak to them. Preach to the soul on the other side of the screen like they are your only assignment—because they might be.

Avoiding Compromise in a Digital Age
The temptation in digital ministry is to trade boldness for applause, conviction for trends, and truth for influence. Guard your heart.

- Do not water down the Gospel to grow your following.

- Do not chase algorithms over the anointing.

- Do not become the focus—keep Jesus front and center.

- Do not fall into fruitless arguments and digital drama.

Stay pure. Stay prayerful. Stay submitted.

Preach the Word. Be unmoved by views. Be faithful to the commission.

"Moreover, it is required in stewards, that a man be found faithful."

(1 Corinthians 4:2)

Testimonies from the Digital Harvest

The Gospel is already reaping online:

- A Facebook post about Jesus led a suicidal teenager to message a believer—and find salvation.

- A TikTok reel about repentance convicted a backslider to return to God.

- A YouTube teaching on the cross brought a Muslim man to Christ in secret.

- A livestream of worship led to deliverance in a living room across the world.

Don't underestimate what God can do with one post, one message, one obedient digital witness.

Final Charge: The World Is Online. So Must the Church Be.

Evangelist—your phone is not just for communication. It's a pulpit. Your camera is not just for selfies. It's a tool to proclaim salvation. Your voice is not just for opinions. It's been filled with fire from the altar.

Preach in pixels. Prophesy in stories. Share Jesus in every space.

The harvest is not only outside—it is online.

You may never meet them in the flesh—but you will see them in eternity. So post. Go live. Create. Preach. Weep. Testify.

Let your light shine—not just in the sanctuary, but on every screen.

Jesus must be known—on every platform, in every language, to every soul.

Let digital evangelism become part of your calling—not for popularity, but for the harvest.

Chapter 11
Follow-Up and Discipleship

From Decision to Discipleship—Raising a Lasting Harvest

One of the great tragedies in modern evangelism is when people are led to Christ—and then left alone. We celebrate decisions, but we neglect discipleship. We shout over hands raised at the altar, but fail to see those same hands weeks later, fading back into the world. The result? Souls that sprouted in fire but withered in isolation.

This is not how Jesus designed His Church.

The Great Commission is not merely a call to preach. It is a call to disciple.

"Go ye therefore, and teach all nations, baptizing them... teaching them to observe all things whatsoever I have commanded you..."

(Matthew 28:19–20)

The goal is not just conversion—it is transformation. Evangelism does not finish at the point of salvation—it begins there. Every soul that receives the Gospel must now be rooted, equipped, nurtured, and trained in the ways of the Kingdom.

Evangelist, if you love people enough to preach to them, then you must also love them enough to walk with them.

Why Follow-Up Matters

When a person comes to Christ, their spirit is made new—but their habits, surroundings, thinking patterns, and emotions often remain unchanged. They have been born again—but like a newborn child, they require nurturing. They need teaching, relationship, and instruction on how to live in this new life.

Jesus warned that some seed falls on shallow soil—where it quickly springs up, but just as quickly withers away because it has no root. **(Matthew 13:20–21)** This is the danger of shallow evangelism: people respond, but no one walks with them.

Follow-up provides roots. It turns moments of decision into movements of discipleship. It creates stability, growth, and lasting fruit.

A newborn baby cannot survive without nourishment. And neither can a newborn believer.

The Essentials of Effective Follow-Up
1. Immediate Contact and Connection

As soon as someone surrenders to Christ—respond. Whether it was an altar call, a street encounter, or an online message, follow up quickly.

- Get their name and contact with love and integrity.

- Let them know: "You are not alone. We are with you."

- Contact them within 24–48 hours if possible. A simple call or text can make the difference between staying and drifting.

They are entering a battle. Don't let them walk into it uncovered. Let your follow-up be pastoral, not just procedural.

2. Personal Encouragement and Assurance

New believers wrestle with questions like:

- "Was I really saved?"

- "Why do I still feel tempted?"

- "What's next?"

Take time to meet with them. Encourage them. Explain what salvation is:

- Their spirit has been made new **(2 Corinthians 5:17).**

- God has sealed them with His Spirit **(Ephesians 1:13).**

- Their feelings may fluctuate—but God's promise is unchanging.

Give them key scriptures:

- **John 1:12 – "But as many as received him..."**

- **Romans 8:1 – "There is therefore now no condemnation..."**

- **Psalm 23 – "The Lord is my Shepherd..."**

- **Philippians 1:6 – "He which hath begun a good work in you..."**

Walk them through what has happened and what is to come. Assure them that God finishes what He starts.

3. Invite Them Into Community

The Church is a family. Don't let them be spiritual orphans. Invite them to:

- Attend Sunday services—not just as guests, but as sons and daughters.

- Join a small group or Bible study.

- Meet other believers who will strengthen their faith.

Assign a mature believer or discipleship partner to check in weekly. This isn't about control—it's about connection. A simple, faithful relationship can anchor a believer during their most vulnerable season.

Let them be known. Let them be loved. Let them belong.

4. Provide Clear Discipleship Pathways

Discipleship doesn't happen by accident. It must be intentional and structured.

Offer:

- A new believer's class (in-person or online).
- A Bible reading plan with simple notes.
- A Spirit-led devotional for daily growth.
- Basic teachings on prayer, the Holy Spirit, holiness, and repentance.
- Conversations about baptism, communion, and church life.

Teach with patience. Define the terms we assume they know. Explain how to pray, how to study, how to resist temptation, and how to walk in purity.

"As newborn babes, desire the sincere milk of the word, that ye may grow thereby."

(1 Peter 2:2)

Give them milk. Teach them truth. Don't rush them—but don't leave them in infancy.

5. Lead Them into Baptism

Baptism is not optional—it's obedience. It is not salvation—but it is a sign of submission and a seal of identification.

"Repent, and be baptized every one of you in the name of Jesus Christ..."
(Acts 2:38)

Teach them what baptism means:

- The burial of the old life.

- The resurrection into new life.

- A public declaration of allegiance to Christ.

Celebrate it publicly. Invite their family and friends. Make baptism a high point, not a side event. Let it mark them forever.

6. Walk With Them—Not Ahead of Them

Discipleship is not a six-week course. It is a lifelong journey. It's messy. It requires patience. Some will stumble. Some will disappear and return. Some will grow fast. Others will crawl.

Walk with grace and truth. Remember how Jesus walked with you.

- Keep reaching out.

- Keep inviting them in.

- Keep calling them to grow.

And when they're strong enough, teach them to disciple others. The cycle continues when the reached become reproducers.

Building a System That Supports the Soul

We must build systems in our churches and ministries that sustain the soul after salvation. Not just celebration, but formation.

This includes:

- Follow-up teams trained to love and listen.

- Printed and digital resources for new believers.

- Tracking spiritual growth—not just headcount.

- Creating space for mentorship and friendship.

- Building atmospheres where the Spirit disciples, convicts, and empowers.

Revival without discipleship is short-lived. Crowds come, but crowds go. If you want lasting harvest, you must root people in the Word and in community.

Jesus discipled twelve. And those twelve shook the world.

A Final Charge: Raise the Soul, Not Just Win It

Evangelist—your assignment does not end when they pray a prayer. That's where the real work begins.

You must see the newborn believer as a soul in transition:

- Out of darkness and into light.

- Out of bondage and into freedom.

- Out of orphanhood and into sonship.

But that transition needs guides. It needs pastors. It needs discipleship.

The devil doesn't back off after the altar call. In fact, he often intensifies his attacks. The seed must be protected. The soul must be tended. The faith must be built.

Jesus didn't just preach to crowds. He sat with His disciples. He explained. He prayed. He corrected. He empowered. He walked with them.

Now, go and do likewise.

Win the soul. Keep the soul. Raise the soul. And send them into the harvest.

Because evangelism is not complete until the one who was won becomes a witness.

Chapter 12
The Rewards and the Cost

The Crown Is Greater Than the Cross You Carry

Evangelism is glorious—and gritty. It's filled with miracles and marked by battle. It brings deep joy—and deep pain. It will stretch you, test you, and transform you. It will cost you popularity, comfort, energy, and sometimes relationships. But it will also bring eternal fruit, holy fire, and divine reward.

Many begin evangelizing with zeal, but when resistance hits, they fall back. They loved the fire of the altar—but not the loneliness after the meeting. They rejoiced at hands raised—but weren't prepared for nights weeping over cold hearts. But hear this: Jesus never said it would be easy. He said it would be worth it.

"If any man will come after me, let him deny himself, and take up his cross daily, and follow me."

(Luke 9:23)

There is a cost. But there is also a crown. And that crown—unseen by man, but promised by Heaven—is worth every sacrifice.

The Reward of Souls

"And they that be wise shall shine as the brightness of the firmament; and they that turn many to righteousness as the stars for ever and ever."

(Daniel 12:3)

There is no greater joy than seeing a soul snatched from death and reborn into life. To watch tears fall at the mention of Jesus. To hear the voice tremble in repentance. To watch hell lose another one.

Every soul you lead to Christ is a miracle. You are not just giving a message—you are participating in Heaven's celebration.

"Likewise, I say unto you, there is joy in the presence of the angels of God over one sinner that repenteth."

(Luke 15:10)

No salary, no applause, no platform can match the eternal reward of a life forever changed. That is your fruit. That is your joy.

The Reward of Pleasing God

"Wherefore we labour, that, whether present or absent, we may be accepted of him. For we must all appear before the judgment seat of Christ..."

(2 Corinthians 5:9–10)

One day, every evangelist will stand before the Lord—not to be judged for sin, but to be rewarded for obedience. On that day, what will matter is not how many followers you had, but how many times you obeyed.

God is not measuring your ministry by crowds or clicks. He is measuring your faithfulness. Did you speak when He said speak? Did you go when He said go? Did you labor for souls even when you were tired, rejected, or alone?

We will not regret being hated. We will regret staying silent.

"Henceforth there is laid up for me a crown of righteousness... and not to me only, but unto all them also that love his appearing."

(2 Timothy 4:8)

Preach with Heaven's smile in mind. Please the One who called you.

The Reward of Eternal Impact

You will not fully know your impact until you stand before Christ. But in that moment, you will see them:

- The girl from the outreach who went on to lead a ministry.
- The man from the hospital who came to Christ on his deathbed.
- The teen who saw your post and surrendered his life.
- The mother who heard your street message and was never the same.

Paul said:

"For what is our hope, or joy, or crown of rejoicing? Are not even ye... in the presence of our Lord Jesus Christ at his coming?"
(1 Thessalonians 2:19)

The souls you reached will become your crown of rejoicing. What you did for one, eternity will never forget.

The Cost: Rejection and Mockery

"And ye shall be hated of all men for my name's sake..."
(Matthew 10:22)

You will be misunderstood. You will be mocked. You will be labeled as extreme, unloving, old-fashioned, or religious. Even some within the Church will say, "That's too much."

But the same crowd that shouted "Hosanna" on Sunday screamed "Crucify Him" on Friday.

Evangelist, you must grow thick skin and a tender heart. Don't preach for approval. Preach from assignment.

"And they departed... rejoicing that they were counted worthy to suffer shame for his name."
(Acts 5:41)

Be honored to bear His reproach. It means you're doing damage to darkness.

The Cost: Spiritual Warfare

To preach the Gospel is to invade enemy territory. When you open your mouth, you pick a fight with hell. The devil does not fear silent saints. But he trembles at a Spirit-filled soul-winner.

You will feel resistance. Confusion. Weariness. Isolation. Doubt. The attack may come through your health, your finances, or your relationships.

But do not fear.

"Greater is he that is in you, than he that is in the world."
(1 John 4:4)

You have authority. Put on the armor **(Ephesians 6:10–18)**. Stay under the blood. Fast. Pray. Speak the Word. Keep your heart clean and your hands lifted.

Warfare is not a sign to quit—it is confirmation that you are effective.

The Cost: Personal Sacrifice

Evangelism costs comfort.

- It will cost you late nights and early mornings.

- It will cost you financially.

- It will cost your schedule, your energy, and your preferences.

It may mean pouring out when you feel empty. It may mean choosing the field over the event. It may mean preaching to a crowd of two when you hoped for two hundred.

But it's worth it.

"And I will very gladly spend and be spent for you..."
(2 Corinthians 12:15)

"He that winneth souls is wise."
(Proverbs 11:30)

You cannot pour into others and remain dry. God will fill the evangelist who continues to pour.

"The liberal soul shall be made fat: and he that watereth shall be watered also himself."
(Proverbs 11:25)

Give your life—and you will find His.

A Final Word: The Crown Is Coming

Evangelist—it is worth it.

Every sleepless night. Every tear. Every prayer. Every seed sown that felt ignored. Every sermon you preached in the street while others passed you by. Every moment you obeyed and wondered if it mattered.

It mattered.

Heaven saw.

Hell trembled.

And the King remembers.

"Well done, thou good and faithful servant... enter thou into the joy of thy lord."
(Matthew 25:21)

That moment is coming. And in that moment, you'll forget the pain. The rejection. The loneliness. The attacks. Because you'll see the faces. You'll hear the stories. You'll wear the crown.

So keep going. Keep burning. Keep preaching.

The cost is real—but the crown is eternal.

Chapter 13
Evangelism and Revival

No Revival Without Reaching the Lost

Revival is not merely emotionalism. It is not long services or prophetic moments alone. Revival is when Heaven touches earth and man responds with repentance, surrender, and fire. True revival disrupts the comfortable, awakens the sleeping, and confronts sin with truth and power. And at the heart of every God-breathed revival is evangelism.

Revival that does not reach the lost is not revival—it is refreshing. Refreshing blesses the believer. Revival rescues the sinner. It doesn't just make the Church shout—it makes the Church go. It doesn't stop at the altar—it spreads to the alley, the avenue, and the addict. It turns passion into proclamation.

Evangelism is not the fruit of revival. Evangelism is the furnace that fuels it. Every true outpouring has come where the Gospel was preached, sinners were confronted, and Jesus was exalted.

The Book of Acts: Revival in Motion

The early Church didn't host revival events—they were the revival. When the Holy Spirit fell in **Acts 2**, Peter did not sit and soak—he stood and preached. Three thousand souls were saved in one day.

In **Acts 3**, after healing a lame man at the gate, Peter used the miracle to declare Christ again. In **Acts 4**, when persecution came, the

Church didn't retreat—they prayed for more boldness, and the place where they gathered shook.

"And with great power gave the apostles witness of the resurrection of the Lord Jesus: and great grace was upon them all." (Acts 4:33)

Every time the Spirit was poured out, evangelism erupted. Preaching followed power. Salvations followed preaching. The Church didn't grow by attraction. It grew by proclamation.

They didn't wait for the world to walk into the upper room—they took the fire into the streets.

Historical Revivals Were Fueled by Evangelism

Throughout Church history, every great move of God was marked by the bold proclamation of the Gospel.

- The First Great Awakening – George Whitefield and Jonathan Edwards preached in fields and churches, calling men to repentance. Crowds trembled under conviction.

- The Second Great Awakening – Charles Finney thundered across cities. Meetings were filled with tears, conversions, and bold altar calls.

- The Welsh Revival (1904–05) – Evan Roberts led prayer gatherings that erupted into street evangelism. Taverns emptied, churches overflowed, and the lost were swept into the Kingdom.

- The Azusa Street Revival (1906) – William Seymour's prayer movement birthed global Pentecostalism. But it didn't stay in a small room—it was carried by fiery evangelists to the nations.

These were not just moves of power—they were movements of harvest. Revival burned hot because evangelism kept feeding the flame.

Evangelism Prepares the Way for Outpouring

We often pray, "Lord, send revival." But God is asking, "Will you go?" When the Church obeys the command to preach, God responds with power. The Gospel provokes the supernatural. Souls pulled from darkness make room for the Holy Spirit to descend.

Isaiah 58 links revival not to song, but to mission:

"If thou draw out thy soul to the hungry, and satisfy the afflicted soul; then shall thy light rise in obscurity..."

(Isaiah 58:10)

When the Church starts feeding the spiritually starving, the light rises. When we give ourselves to the broken, the revival glory comes. Evangelism makes space for divine visitation.

Revival is not only something we pray for—it is something we prepare for through obedience.

Revival Awakens the Church to the Lost

One of the purest signs of true revival is a Church that can no longer be comfortable with the lost going to hell.

Revival shatters apathy. It reawakens urgency. The revived believer does not simply want deeper teaching—they want souls. They are not chasing signs—they are chasing the harvest.

They begin to:

- Cry in prayer for the prodigal.

- Speak boldly to strangers.

- Witness without fear of rejection.

- Burn to see the unsaved repent.

True revival moves the Church from passivity to pursuit. It creates a people who are not content with good meetings—they want to see lives transformed.

When revival is real, evangelism is relentless.

Evangelism Sustains Revival

Revival that does not reach beyond the walls will die within them. You can't contain fire without feeding it. You can't keep the glory without guarding the mission.

Evangelism is the fuel of revival.

When people are being saved:

- The Church stays on its knees.

- Worship becomes warfare.

- Preaching stays urgent.

- The atmosphere remains holy.

- A spirit of repentance lingers.

- The fear of the Lord increases.

A soul-winning church is a revival-sustaining church. As long as we keep reaching for the lost, God keeps releasing the glory.

If you want longevity in revival, raise up laborers, not just intercessors. Train evangelists, not just singers. Send witnesses, not just waiters.

Revival Is Here—Now Go Preach

You don't need a tent, a pulpit, or a microphone to release revival. You need obedience.

- Preach in the streets.
- Pray in the hospital.
- Share in your workplace.
- Lay hands on the addicted.
- Speak to the outcast.
- Host home meetings.
- Weep for your neighborhood.

The fire is not reserved for platforms. It is reserved for the obedient.
"And how shall they hear without a preacher? And how shall they preach, except they be sent?"
(Romans 10:14–15)
You've been sent. You are the revival. Don't wait for the next event. Be the next eruption.

Final Charge: Revival and Evangelism Are One River

Evangelist—if you want fire, preach the Gospel.

If you want outpouring, reach the lost.

If you want glory, step into the harvest.

Let your voice carry the thunder of eternity. Let your feet run with urgency. Let your tears become intercession. Let your life become the proof that revival is not a theory—it is a person on fire.

You are that fire.

You are that spark.

You are the move of God your city is waiting for.

When evangelism meets revival, the result is cities shaken, souls saved, and Jesus glorified. This is the river that makes glad the city of God.

Chapter 14
Raising Up Evangelists

Multiplying the Voice That Shakes Hell

The future of evangelism is not in one voice—it's in many. While God uses individuals mightily, His long-term strategy has always been multiplication. Jesus didn't just win souls—He raised soul-winners. He didn't cling to His mission—He commissioned others to carry it. And He gave a pattern that the Church must follow today.

"The harvest truly is great, but the labourers are few: pray ye therefore the Lord of the harvest, that he would send forth labourers into his harvest."

(Luke 10:2)

The cry of Heaven in every generation is this: Send more workers. Send men and women who burn with the Gospel. Raise up bold witnesses—not just from platforms, but from prayer closets, job sites, universities, and street corners. If we are going to see nations shaken and regions transformed, we must not only evangelize—we must multiply evangelists.

The Evangelist Is a Gift, Not a Guest

Many churches are built around the shepherd, the teacher, and the prophet—but the evangelist is often neglected, misunderstood, or invited in as an occasional guest speaker. This is not how Christ intended His Church to function.

"And he gave some, apostles; and some, prophets; and some, evangelists; and some, pastors and teachers; for the perfecting of the saints, for the work of the ministry..."

(Ephesians 4:11–12)

The evangelist is not a rogue operator. He or she is a gift from Christ to the Church—for equipping, training, igniting, and sending. Their job is not just to preach a message—it's to stir the Church into movement. It is to make soul-winning normal, not rare.

Leaders, we must make space for the evangelist. Celebrate their fire. Give them responsibility. Allow them to train. Let them release outreach teams. Let them raise up others who carry the Gospel with clarity and conviction.

A church that raises evangelists becomes a threat to darkness and a magnet for harvest.

Training Evangelists in Word and Power

Evangelists don't emerge fully developed. They must be trained, tested, and equipped—not just in passion, but in purity and power. The call is holy. The warfare is real. The responsibility is weighty.

Evangelists must be trained in:

- The Gospel – To preach with clarity and doctrinal accuracy.

- Scripture – To ground their message in eternal truth.

- Prayer and fasting – To carry supernatural power and spiritual discernment.

- Boldness – To speak truth in love without fear of man.

- Demonstration – To minister in healing, deliverance, and prophetic gifts.

- Discipleship – To follow up and care for those they reach.

- Humility and accountability – To finish well and avoid compromise.

Create intentional environments where evangelists are:
- Refined by the Word
- Strengthened in community
- Empowered by the Spirit
- Corrected with love
- Released in obedience

Give them platforms to practice, spaces to grow, and mentors to sharpen them. Evangelists flourish in fire and fellowship.

Recognizing the Evangelistic Gift

Many believers carry the evangelistic gift long before they realize it. They may not have a pulpit—but they carry a burden. They share Christ naturally. They feel grief when others reject the Gospel. They care deeply for souls others ignore.

Leaders, you must discern the fire:
- Do they light up when talking about reaching the lost?
- Do they speak boldly even in simple settings?
- Are they constantly inviting, praying, and compelling others toward Jesus?

Call it out. Speak life over it. Invest in it. Don't let it sit dormant. Discipleship means drawing the evangelist out of the shadows and into their assignment.

Give them books. Let them shadow experienced leaders. Invite them to street ministry. Watch how they respond to the altar. Pay attention to the tears when the Gospel is preached. These are the markers of a soul-winner in the making.

Don't Sit on the Evangelist—Send Them

One of the greatest failures of the modern Church has been to recognize evangelists—but never release them.

Jesus raised disciples to go. Paul trained Timothy to go. Philip was sent to Samaria and then to the desert road. Evangelists were never meant to be ornaments—they are arrows. They are not meant to be retained—they are meant to be released.

Let them:

- Preach

- Launch evangelistic ministries

- Lead street and school outreaches

- Plant Gospel hubs

- Start digital evangelism platforms

- Go to the nations

You may lose them from your building—but you will gain souls for eternity. You may not keep them in the pew—but you will hear their echo in the harvest fields.

Train them. Trust them. Send them.

Create a Culture That Multiplies Evangelists

Raising one evangelist is good. Raising generations is better. This requires a culture—not just a moment.

A multiplying culture:

- Holds regular evangelism trainings.

- Creates weekly outreach opportunities.

- Highlights testimonies of salvation.

- Publicly commissions new soul-winners.

- Provides mentorship and accountability.

- Creates low-pressure platforms where young evangelists can preach, share, and grow.

If you build the altar, God will send the fire. If you make room, God will send the laborers.

Pastors, make it part of your leadership pipeline. Youth leaders, train teens to preach. Small group leaders, equip your group to witness. This is how evangelism becomes DNA, not just decoration.

Final Charge: Multiply the Mission

Evangelist—your calling is not only to reach the lost. It is to raise the army. To equip, to impart, to mobilize. The harvest is too vast for one voice. We need an uprising of preachers, teachers, street ministers, digital witnesses, intercessors, and Gospel messengers.

"And the things that thou hast heard of me among many witnesses, the same commit thou to faithful men, who shall be able to teach others also."

(2 Timothy 2:2)

Don't let the fire die with you. Don't bury the mantle. Pass it on. Mentor. Pour out. Impart. Reproduce.

This is the Kingdom pattern:

- Win one.

- Train one.

- Send one.

- Repeat.

Until the whole world hears. Until every street, village, and screen is filled with the Gospel. Until Jesus comes.

Chapter 15
The Urgency of the Hour

This Is the Final Lap—Run to Win

Time is not on our side. The window is closing. The harvest is ripening—but so is judgment. We are not promised another decade, another year, or even another day. The Gospel is not a suggestion—it is a command. And that command carries urgency.

"I must work the works of him that sent me, while it is day: the night cometh, when no man can work."
(John 9:4)

Jesus felt the weight of time—and so must we. The night is coming. Eternity is not far off. And while the Church debates, delays, and entertains—the world is dying. We cannot afford to wait. We must preach now, pray now, reach now.

This is not the hour for hesitation. It is the hour for fire. The alarm of Heaven is sounding—and evangelists must rise.

Eternity Is Real—And Closer Than We Think

"And as it is appointed unto men once to die, but after this the judgment..."
(Hebrews 9:27)

Every person you pass on the street will one day stand before God. Every barista, every classmate, every co-worker, every neighbor—they will either be welcomed into eternal joy or cast into eternal judgment.

Hell is not a myth. It is not metaphorical. It is a real place of unending torment, separation, and regret. It was created for the devil and his angels—but every person who rejects Christ is choosing it.

If you truly believe in eternity, you cannot be casual. You must speak. You must warn. You must weep. You must rescue.

"Knowing therefore the terror of the Lord, we persuade men..."

(2 Corinthians 5:11)

Every moment matters. Every soul counts. And we do not get to decide when the door closes.

The Spirit Is Moving—Don't Miss the Moment

This is not just a dangerous hour—it is a divine hour. The Holy Spirit is brooding over the earth. Hearts are being stirred. Doors are opening. Miracles are happening. God is calling.

You were born for this. You are not an accident. You are a voice, a vessel, a trumpet in the hand of the Lord.

"Who knoweth whether thou art come to the kingdom for such a time as this?"

(Esther 4:14)

Now is that time. The Spirit is moving. But He will not drag you—He will invite you. You must say yes. You must move when He says move. There is a remnant rising—but you must decide whether you will be among them.

This is not the time to be cute. This is not the time to be cautious. This is the time to be dangerous to hell.

Delayed Obedience Is Disobedience
"To him that knoweth to do good, and doeth it not, to him it is sin."
(James 4:17)

Excuses don't exempt us from responsibility. Delay is still disobedience. Many are called—but few move.

Why?

- "I'm not ready."

- "I don't know enough."

- "I'll wait until I'm older."

- "What will people think?"

These are the voices of fear, comfort, and compromise. They are the lies that silence lions. But God is not looking for qualified—He is looking for available. He doesn't anoint perfection. He anoints obedience.

You don't need more confirmation—you need conviction. You don't need another prophecy—you need boldness.

The Gospel is urgent. The Spirit is ready. The lost are dying. Now is the time.

Jesus Is Coming Soon
The Church must return to this truth: Jesus is returning. And He is not coming back for a sleepy, silent people—but for a bride who has made herself ready.

"This same Jesus... shall so come in like manner as ye have seen him go into heaven."
(Acts 1:11)

He is coming:
- Not as a teacher, but as a judge.
- Not as a lamb, but as a lion.
- Not to call men to repentance—but to reward the righteous and punish the wicked.

When He comes, it will be too late to evangelize. Too late to repent. Too late to preach.

That day is near. The signs are clear. The earth groans. The heavens declare it. And the Spirit is crying out, "Who will go for Us?"

Final Charge: This Is the Hour—You Are the Voice
"The time is short..."
(1 Corinthians 7:29)

You may not have a stage. You may not have a following. But you have a voice—and a mandate from Heaven.

- You don't need to be famous. You need to be faithful.
- You don't need to be a theologian. You need to be filled.
- You don't need a platform. You need passion.
- You don't need to go viral. You need to go boldly.

"Preach the word; be instant in season, out of season..."
(2 Timothy 4:2)

Preach like it's your last sermon.
Witness like their soul depends on it—because it does.
Pray like time is running out—because it is.
Stand in the gap. Blow the trumpet. Shake the gates.

And when the day comes—when you stand before the King—you won't regret what it cost. You'll only regret when you stayed silent.

Let This Be Your Anthem
"I did not delay.//
I did not stay quiet.

I did not wait for perfect timing.

I ran. I preached. I wept. I reached.

And now—I lay my crown at His feet."

The hour is urgent.

The harvest is ready.

Hell is real.

Eternity is forever.

And the Gospel is still the power of God unto salvation.

Evangelist—run.

Evangelist—burn.

Evangelist—go.

While there is still time.

30 Powerful Principles for Evangelists Traveling to Preach

Spirit-Filled, Practical, and Character-Building Wisdom for the Road

Evangelists are not just speakers—they are messengers. When you travel to minister in churches, cities, or nations, you carry more than a sermon. You carry the fragrance of Christ, the Word of the Lord, and the weight of your calling. But with that privilege comes responsibility.

Here are 30 principles—practical, biblical, and Spirit-filled—that will keep your character strong, your heart pure, and your ministry fruitful as you travel to preach the Gospel:

1. Take an Offering Boldly—Without Manipulation

Never apologize for receiving an offering. Jesus said the laborer is worthy of his wages **(Luke 10:7)**. Present the opportunity to give, not pressure to comply. Trust the Spirit—not guilt—to move hearts.

2. Pay for Your Own Travel When You Can

If you're able, cover your own costs. This shows that you're coming to serve, not to be served. It demonstrates honor and maturity, and opens the door for unexpected blessing.

3. Bring an Offering With You

Don't arrive with an empty hand. Come prepared to sow into the house that receives you. Honor unlocks favor—and sowing where you're fed brings a double harvest.

4. Don't Be a Diva

You're not a celebrity. You're a vessel. Keep your ego in check. The moment you think the ministry is about you is the moment you begin to drift from your true assignment.

5. Be Low Maintenance

The less you demand, the more God can surprise you. Be flexible. Be grateful. Be willing to sleep on a couch if needed. Jesus had no place to lay His head—neither should you be obsessed with comfort.

6. Preach the Word, Not Your Brand

People don't need your personality—they need the Person of Jesus Christ. Don't use the pulpit to promote your image. Lift up the cross, not your logo.

7. Honor the Pastor in Public and Private

Never correct or rebuke the house publicly. If there are concerns, share them privately and humbly. Your job is to strengthen the leadership, not undermine it.

8. Submit to the Flow of the House

Respect time limits, cultural rhythms, and house rules. If you're asked to preach for 30 minutes—preach for 28. Submission is not weakness—it's wisdom.

9. Be a Blessing Off the Platform

Ministry doesn't end when the mic is off. Shake hands. Pray for people. Be present. Be approachable. Don't hide in green rooms while souls are hungry for connection.

10. Stay Out of Drama and Church Politics

Don't get entangled in internal issues unless explicitly invited to speak into them. You are there as a guest, not a fixer. Stay focused on your assignment.

11. Don't Flirt or Be Inappropriate

Guard your heart and your conduct. The anointing does not excuse carnality. Keep your eyes, speech, and boundaries holy. Don't let your flesh destroy your witness.

12. Don't Criticize or Compare

Never say, "At the last church I was at..." You're not there to compare—you're there to minister. Be present. Be honoring. Every house is different. Love them where they are.

13. Don't Be Weird About Honorariums

Whatever is given, receive it with grace. God is your source—not the offering envelope. Never preach for a check. Preach for souls.

14. Stay Off Your Phone in the Service

Engage in worship. Lean into the Word. Don't scroll through social media while others are pressing into God's presence. Your reverence matters.

15. Dress Honorably, Not Distractingly

You don't need to wear designer labels or impress anyone. Dress with honor. Be clean, modest, and presentable. Represent the Kingdom well.

16. Don't Promote Yourself from the Pulpit

This is not the time to market your ministry. Don't drop your social media handles between Scriptures. Let your fruit speak for you.

17. Be Early, Not Late

Tardiness dishonors the platform. Arrive early. Pray beforehand. Be ready in spirit and in heart. Don't make others wait on your obedience.

18. Keep Your Hotel Room Holy

Your private space must remain sacred. Don't fill it with carnal entertainment. Don't invite temptation in through compromise. Guard your purity.

19. Don't Overstay After the Assignment

Leave with grace when the work is done. Don't linger for attention or perks. Be a blessing—not a burden. Finish well and move on.

20. Be Honest About Your Finances

If you have financial needs, share them with integrity. Don't guilt people into giving. Let your life be marked by transparency and trust.

21. Fast and Pray Before You Go

Don't bring stale bread to a hungry people. Seek God before you travel. Come carrying fresh fire—not just a recycled sermon.

22. Preach with Fire and Leave with Grace

Don't stand around fishing for compliments. Preach what God gave you, bless the people, and go with joy and humility.

23. Send a Thank-You Message After You Leave

Gratitude is powerful. Send a text or card to thank the host. Appreciation seals assignments. It also leaves a door open for future partnership.

24. Don't Collect Contacts to Recruit Members

You're not there to fish in another man's pond. Don't secretly invite people to your events, church, or email list. That's dishonorable.

25. Keep the Altar Ministry Sacred

Don't rush the work of the Holy Spirit. Don't turn deliverance into drama. Minister with discernment and reverence. Let God move without interruption.

26. Discern the Atmosphere—Don't Perform

Don't force your sermon. Don't perform. Tune your spirit to what God is doing in the room. Flow with the river of the Spirit.

27. Ask the Holy Spirit for the Right Offering Moment

Timing matters. There is a moment for giving that aligns with God's Spirit. Don't force the giving moment—flow with it.

28. Don't Beg—Expect

You're not a beggar. You're a child of the King. Ask, present, and trust God to provide. Never manipulate. Never grovel.

29. Avoid Name-Dropping or Platform Flaunting

You don't need to mention where you've been or who you know. You're not there to impress—you're there to impact.

30. Never Forget—You're a Voice, Not the Star

You are a trumpet for the Gospel. A servant of Jesus. Stay broken. Stay faithful. Stay yielded. Let Christ be seen—not you.

31-Day Evangelist's Reading Plan: "Burning for the Lost"

WEEK 1: The Heart of the Evangelist

1. Luke 15 – The joy of finding the lost.

Focus: God's heart for one soul.

Challenge: Pray for 3 people you know who need salvation.

2. John 3 – You must be born again.

Focus: The foundation of salvation.

Challenge: Practice explaining salvation simply.

3. Isaiah 6 – Send me.

Focus: The call to go.

Challenge: Say yes to God again in prayer.

4. Romans 1 – I'm not ashamed of the Gospel.

Focus: Boldness to preach Christ.

Challenge: Post one Scripture publicly today.

5. Acts 1:1–11 – Power to be a witness.

Focus: Depend on the Holy Spirit.

Challenge: Pray in the Spirit for 15 minutes.

6. Matthew 9:35–38 – The harvest is great.

Focus: Seeing the crowds like Jesus does.

Challenge: Go out and talk to one person about Jesus.

7. 2 Timothy 4:1–8 – Do the work of an evangelist.

Focus: Preach with urgency and endurance.

Challenge: Share your testimony with someone today.

WEEK 2: The Message of the Gospel

8. 1 Corinthians 15:1–11 – The Gospel in full.

Focus: Christ died, was buried, and rose again.

Challenge: Write out the Gospel in 3 sentences.

9. Romans 3 – All have sinned.

Focus: The universality of sin.

Challenge: Ask someone, "Do you think you're a good person?"

10. Romans 5 – Christ died for the ungodly.

Focus: Salvation is undeserved mercy.

Challenge: Thank God for saving you and reach out to another.

11. Romans 6 – Dead to sin, alive in Christ.

Focus: The power of the resurrection.

Challenge: Share how Jesus changed you.

12. Romans 10 – Faith comes by hearing.

Focus: Preaching is essential.

Challenge: Send a Gospel voice note or text today.

13. Ephesians 2 – Saved by grace through faith.

Focus: Not works, but grace.

Challenge: Pray for boldness to explain grace to someone confused about religion.

14. John 10 – The Good Shepherd calls His sheep.

Focus: Jesus draws people by name.

Challenge: Listen for who God is calling near you.

WEEK 3: Evangelism in Action

15. Acts 2 – Peter preaches, 3,000 saved.

Focus: Preach with boldness and truth.

Challenge: Declare the Gospel clearly to someone.

16. Acts 3–4 – Power, healing, and boldness.

Focus: Miracles open doors for the message.

Challenge: Pray for someone to be healed.

17. Acts 8 – Philip and the Ethiopian.

Focus: Be led by the Spirit to one soul.

Challenge: Ask God to lead you to a divine appointment today.

18. Acts 10 – The Gospel crosses cultures.

Focus: Don't limit who God will reach.

Challenge: Share the Gospel with someone different than you.

19. Acts 13 – Paul's first missionary journey.

Focus: Sent by the Spirit, not self.

Challenge: Ask God where He wants to send you.

20. Acts 16 – Paul and Silas in prison.

Focus: Evangelize in every season.

Challenge: Worship in hardship, and share Christ anyway.

21. Acts 17 – Preaching to thinkers and skeptics.

Focus: Contextual evangelism.

Challenge: Share Jesus in a relatable way today.

WEEK 4: Endurance and Eternal Impact

22. 2 Corinthians 4 – We do not lose heart.

Focus: Don't give up, even when rejected.

Challenge: Pray for strength to endure.

23. Galatians 6 – Don't grow weary.

Focus: You will reap if you don't quit.

Challenge: Follow up with someone you've ministered to before.

24. Matthew 24 – The Gospel will be preached.

Focus: End-time urgency.

Challenge: Share the Gospel like Jesus is coming soon.

25. Revelation 7 – Every tribe and tongue.

Focus: Global harvest.

Challenge: Pray for a nation you've never evangelized in.

26. 1 Peter 3:13–17 – Be ready to give an answer.

Focus: Be prepared with words and character.

Challenge: Study one apologetics point today.

27. 1 Thessalonians 2 – The soul-winner's joy.

Focus: People are your crown.

Challenge: Text or call someone you've led to Christ and encourage them.

28. 2 Timothy 2 – Endure hardship as a good soldier.

Focus: Suffering is part of the call.

Challenge: Renew your commitment to the calling today.

29. Jude 20–23 – Snatch them from the fire.

Focus: Rescue and mercy.

Challenge: Pray with burden for the lost today—cry out for them.

30. Psalm 126 – Those who sow in tears will reap in joy.

Focus: The cost and reward of evangelism.

Challenge: Write down what evangelism has cost you—and thank God for it.

31. Mark 16 – Go into all the world.

Focus: This is still the commission.

Challenge: Make a new commitment to go and preach the Gospel, starting today.

Author's Page

Abraham JT Harris was born in Phoenix, Arizona and raised in Buckeye, Arizona. He now serves as the lead pastor of Risen Life Church in Salem, Oregon. In addition to his pastoral work, he is the president of a Bible school and founder of The Roar Ministry—a multifaceted ministry that includes a podcast focused on teaching, news, and empowerment, a publishing company, and a vibrant evangelistic outreach.

Abraham enjoys working out, swimming, and spending time in the great outdoors, but his deepest passion is the work of the ministry—equipping people to walk in truth, power, and purpose.

His life verse is:

"I would have lost heart, unless I had believed that I would see the goodness of the Lord in the land of the living."

—Psalm 27:13 (NKJV)

Made in United States
Troutdale, OR
05/27/2025